A to Z of Taylor Swift

An Alphabetical Journey Through Her Life and Music.

HANNAH KURRY

A is for albums, so many and bright,
Taylor's music, a pure delight.

B IS FOR BANJO, HER COUNTRY START,

Strumming her way into every heart.

C

is for Cats, her feline friends.

Furry purry love, that never ends.

D IS FOR DANCING, TWIRLING AWAY,
On stage and in life, come what may..

E IS FOR EASTER EGGS, HIDDEN IN PLAIN SIGHT,

CLUES IN HER LYRICS BRING FANS DELIGHT.

F

F is for **Fans**, loyal and true,

Cheering for Taylor in all that she'll do.

G IS FOR GRAMMYS,
SHINING SO BRIGHT,
AWARDS FOR HER TALENT,
EARNED NIGHT AFTER NIGHT.

H is for hits, one after another, songs that unite us, like sisters and brothers.

I is for imagination, wild and free,
building whole worlds in her melody.

J IS FOR JULY

THE MONTH OF
HER BIRTH,
WHEN A STAR
WAS BORN
TO SHARE HER
WORTH.

K is

is for kindness,
She spreads it wide,
helping her fans
with love as a guide.

L is for Lover,

A song and a glow,
A celebration of love,
as her stories grow.

M is for Music,

her life and her heart,
a passion and gift
from the very start.

N

is for **Nashville,**
where it
began,
a young girl's
dream
turned into
a plan.

O is for outfit, sparkling and bright,
changing with every song in the night.

P is for performance, grand and bold,
a show full of wonder, a story told.

Q IS FOR

QUEEN OF MUSIC AND ART, TAYLOR REIGNS SUPREME, STRAIGHT FROM THE HEART.

R is for **Red**, an album so dear,
Love, loss, and passion, bringing us near.

S IS FOR SWIFTIES,
LOYAL AND TRUE,
HER BIGGEST SUPPORTERS IN ALL THAT THEY DO.

T is for Taylor

a name we adore,
a storyteller whose
songs we explore.

V is for videos, her stories on screen,
bringing her lyrics to life like a dream.

U

is for umbrella,
For rain or shine,
Taylor stays graceful,
her style divine.

X IS FOR XOXO,
HUGS AND LOVE,
TAYLOR SENDS
KINDNESS FROM
BELOW AND ABOVE.

W is for Willow,
swaying and strong,
a melody flowing like
life's own
song.

Y IS FOR FOR YOU, HER FANS SO DEAR, A BOND THAT GROWS STRONGER STRONGER AFTER YEAR.

Z is for Zenith,

The peak of her fame,
Taylor's a legend in music and name.